Living Outside The Box

(A Peckham Parable)

BOB HURLEY

Published in 2006 in the UK
by Comfort Books
PO Box 3937
Bath
BA1 0BR
www.comfortbooks.co.uk

ISBN
0-9551874-1-9
978-0-9551874-1-4

British Library Cataloguing Publication Data
A catalogue record for this book is available
from the British Library.

Illustrations by John Byrne
Book design by Sarah Heppenstall

Printed by Advance Book Printing

This is the story of All Saints Church written from my point of view. Others may view things from a different angle and perspective. There were many other adventures that took place during the six years that we were there, and lots of different characters involved – all of whom I would like to thank, even if they are not mentioned in this book. At the end of the day all that matters is that God did it, and the church itself remains living proof of this.

This Book is dedicated to:

Mavis, who believed with me,
Jane, who stood strong with me,
And my Latin teacher, who said I'd never write a book

I would like to thank John Byrne for doing all the illustrations for this book. He was a member of All Saints during the time that I was ministering there, and is very much a part of this story.

Contents

Preface

From the moment we arrive on the planet, we are
exposed to boundaries. Some are there for our
protection, and for the protection of those around
us, others merely serve to begin a life long process of
restricting our belief in what is possible for us to achieve.

*'Sticks and stones may break my bones, but words can crush
my spirit.'*

We are led to believe that there are things that we can
do, and things that we simply can't. This building of
boundaries is often started, albeit unwittingly, by our
parents, and is continued by our teachers, and school
friends. This process continues throughout our lives,
perhaps reinforced by our exam results, appearance,
or health. It is perhaps reinforced by those senior to us
at work, those with whom we work, the structures and
strategies in our work place – day by day, the building
of boundaries continues, until, sooner or later, the day
comes when we need no one else to restrict our spirits, for
we have begun to believe it and to do it for ourselves. We
become the ones who say no to ourselves.

However what if, one day, you decided to throw off all that hinders you, believe, and go for it with everything you have. Who could then predict what may happen in your life?

My prayer is that this book will start you believing and thinking beyond the boundaries.

"The story of the Church in Peckham is that of a series of chained doors being opened." – Mark Birchall

A Peckham Parable

1. It only takes a spark to start a fire.

Can anything good come from Peckham?   Most people, when they hear the word 'Peckham' immediately think of 'Del boy' from the popular T.V. series 'Only fools and horses', or perhaps on a more serious note, the recent murder of the little boy, Damilola Taylor. Most people have never been there. (It's not a place that has a 'tourist information centre', gourmet restaurants or fine hotels.) It is a place of contrasts: there are colourful parts, and dark parts, such as the North Peckham estate where even the police did not enter lightly, and when they do, only in twos!

It is certainly a place of enormous cultural and racial diversity. A walk down the high street, with its halal butchers, African wig shops, and Caribbean vegetable sellers reveals that. There is poverty, racial tension (not just between black and white!), as well as a new interest shown by young middle class white families, who have worked out that a house there costs the same as a flat in Clapham, and is only twenty minutes away from the centre of town by over line rail. The government has poured millions and millions of pounds into improving the area, yet it still has the air of a place that needs more spending on it, or scrapping and starting all over again. It feels as if it would remain unfinished, no matter how much you spent on it. The truth is that it is a place undergoing great change, trying to become something, but hasn't yet decided what.

Faith wise, it must be one of the most interesting places to minister in the U.K. a fact illustrated by the enormous variety of churches to be found, each one reflecting a different facet of the amazing fusion of cultures to be found in the area. In fact, as you walk down the high street, you are hit by the sheer number of churches; some meeting over shops, others in halls, some promising miracles, others advertising their powerful services - I even saw one promising visas and children! Then there are the few established denominations, some of whose buildings certainly look as if they have seen better days. It was into that category that All Saints Church definitely fell.

All Saints Church was built in the Victorian period, of a humble Kentish ragstone. There was nothing fancy about it, externally it was all overgrown, giving a very convincing impersonation of a redundant church. The congregation had sunk to an all time low of around 20, predominantly elderly people, with most members being of Caribbean descent.

An appropriate sign outside it would have read 'To be demolished'. Dilapidated buildings, disheartened congregation and depleted finances: what could the Church of England do but demolish it? It wasn't viable – that's why they had cut the minister's post to half time. The only sensible thing to do with it was to knock it down. This church was dying, it was finished, a huge liability, with nothing going on that could possibly change things. However, little did they know, there was something happening at All Saints; it happened every Thursday evening, come wind, rain or hail, and it involved a handful of elderly ladies. So what, you might say; what difference could a handful of elderly ladies make? Well that all depends on what they are doing. Prayer is the spark that has lit many great fires throughout history. What these ladies were doing was praying, and where there is prayer, there is hope! Unbeknown to these five ladies, God had heard their prayers and had already begun to move.

2. An unusual move

Usually, the 'done thing' (if you have the chance) is to move out of the dirty, smoky, noisy, violent city into the lovely countryside. We were lucky, we had made it to the nice clean Devonshire countryside, where our kids were in a good state school. I had been working in the diocese of Exeter in the area of church growth, travelling around the countryside, visiting churches and exploring with them how they might reach people around them who didn't go to Church. We lived in our own house, on the outskirts of Plymouth, and were really quite comfortable. However, Jesus never directly spoke about our call to be 'comfortable', and I was about to find out that we were going to remain so for a limited period only.

My wife, Jane, and I were not looking to move. We were settled as a family. Ordinary parish ministry was not something that I ever really wanted to do. A college friend remembers me saying that I would never be a parish priest. It's a dangerous thing to make statements like these without checking with God first, as I was soon to find out.

It all started one day, when a good friend of mine noticed an advert in a Church newspaper, which spoke about a church in inner city London, which needed a vicar. As I read the advert, I thought to myself, "Well I wish them all the best in their search!" The next day, a letter arrived, from another friend, who had cut out the ad, and sent it to me with the words "What about this?" It was a phone call from yet another person on the same theme that caused me to think that perhaps the Lord was trying to get my attention. So I felt that I ought to do something.

With such adverts, the correct procedure is to write to the archdeacon for details, send in a C.V., wait to be short listed, and then attend an interview. Instead of doing this, I looked up the phone number of the local bishop, and phoned him up. To my surprise I actually got to speak to him directly, having been spared the super efficient secretary. I asked him if there were any possibilities with this church. He had obviously never had things put this way before, and asked me what I meant by this. I replied that I believed in church growth, and wanted to know if he thought that this rather dilapidated church could burst into life and growth and vitality.

A week later, I was surprised to find that I had been offered an interview.

3. The interview

The day for the interview came, and I remember driving through the lovely Devonshire countryside, with my wife, Jane, only to end up in Peckham. What a culture shock! Dirty grey concrete houses, noisy, crowded streets. Schools that looked like prisons, and rubbish spilling out of the dustbins onto the pavement. Coming from Devon, with its almost completely homogenous make up, we were suddenly confronted by a mixture of people who looked as if they had been drawn from all corners of the earth. People seemed to be just hanging around on street corners, waiting for something to happen, or for someone 'to happen' to come along. There had been several shootings and muggings in the area, and the whole place seemed menacing and rather dangerous. So dangerous that we were later told that we couldn't live in the existing vicarage, which was next to the church, because 'there would be no one to hear us scream.' This was a real encouragement for a couple with four young children considering coming into the area.

We were herded into a minibus, together with the other interviewees, and shown around the area. Then we were taken to the vicarage, which wasn't the vicarage at all. It was a seven mile round trip from the Church, which in London is a long way, and wasn't even in the same deanery. We knew that we would be too squashed to fit comfortably into this house, and really couldn't wait to get back home to Devon.

Lunch came and went, and the time came for the interview, or should I say, interviews. I once saw on a poster, the following: *'For God so loved the world that He didn't send a committee.'* That afternoon we had to face three separate committees!

The diocese was trying to save money, and as a result was forever cutting posts. In the case of All Saints, Peckham, they had reduced the post to half time, combining it with another, recently reduced, half time post – that of Deanery Missioner. The idea of this post was to help the other seven churches in the Deanery (Anglican speak for a group of churches in an area) in the area of mission. This side of the job had attracted me as it seemed that I would be able to build on my experiences in the Exeter Diocese. I went to the deanery interview first, and had a nice enough chat with them, but we didn't get down to talking about what they really meant by the word 'Mission'. I later discovered that the reason for this was that the churches themselves couldn't agree on what mission was all about. So this rather nebulous job never really existed in a meaningful way.

The next committee was the Diocesan Development committee. It was quite a high powered one, with both the bishop and the Archdeacon present. Its aim was to speak about the Church Development Plan. It turned out that Development was just a euphemism for Demolition. The general idea was to knock down the church, the church hall, and the vicarage, and build private housing on the plot. Included in this scheme would be a small multi-function community hall to house the residual congregation of around 20. Needless to say, the project would have brought quite a tidy sum into the diocesan coffers. Speaking with the other interviewees, it had become plain that, unlike me, they all had previous experience in the area of buildings and development. This committee wanted to know if I understood their plan. I did. However understanding a thing is different to agreeing with it. The boundaries were very much in place!

The final interview of the afternoon was with the representatives from the church itself. I remember going into a room with them and saying: "there is only one thing that I want to ask you, do you believe that God can fill this church?" They were a little stunned, they paused a moment then said, "Yes we do, we just need someone to lead us." When they said these words, something moved in my heart. I forgot about the area, the schools, the size of the accommodation, and the fact that I had never been a vicar before, (and never wanted to be one!) and suddenly found myself saying that I would love to come and build the church with them.

At the end of a long day, we returned to our house in Devon, walked through the door, only to hear the phone ring. My wife answered it. It was the bishop, who asked me if I wanted the job. I said, "Yes," and spent the rest of the evening wondering what I had done.

A couple of weeks later the bishop retired.

4. Head on the chopping block

We moved into the Deanery Missioner's house in September, just in time for the start of term. Almost immediately Jane and I began to meet and pray with people in the Church. Some had thought that the plan for demolition was the only way forward. The new multipurpose hall would be easy to heat, cheap to run, and they could still have their weekly services in it. It made a lot of sense. However God is the one who raises our expectations, and can do far more that we hope for or can possibly imagine. Slowly but surely, people began to believe that instead of knocking down the existing church, we should oppose the development plan, and believe that God could fill the huge cold barn of a church that was All Saints. A sense of optimism and excitement began to grow among the church members. However I was soon to find out that this was not shared by everyone concerned.

In the Church of England, you are offered a post, and when you accept it you are given a moving grant. You move into the new vicarage, get settled, and a couple of weeks later you are licensed. It is only when you have your licence that you have your job. We had moved, and people were now beginning to talk about the exciting new idea. However we were in the position where we had left our last job, moved house, but had not yet been licensed. This is usually a very straightforward process, but that afternoon I found myself suddenly put on the spot.

We were putting up some shelves in the dining room when we heard a knock at the door. I went to open the door and there was one of the diocesan officials from the interview committee, that is the development committee. He came into the front room with a very serious look on his face. It turned out that the diocese was very keen on the demolition plan, very keen indeed, and had already spent several thousand pounds on architects plans with an expensive London firm. Word had by now got around about the change in direction that the church was taking and it was obvious that I was the orchestrator. I was asked to explain what was happening.

I stated plainly my belief that God could fill All Saints Church with believers, and that it was not His will to knock it down. He challenged me on this and I refused to budge. Therefore, seeing that this 'little chat' was not working, he said that if I would not change my mind, it was doubtful that the diocese would license me. This was the defining moment for me; did I really believe what I was saying to people? Would I be willing to stake everything on this belief? I looked at my wife, then

turned to him and said, "Well don't license me then."
This was clearly the wrong answer. He said that he was
going to the bishop immediately, and left the house in
such a hurry that this very organised man left his jacket
and diary behind.

A couple of hours later the phone rang, and I found
myself summoned to the bishop's palace. After a brief
wait, and the thought of how much better his house
would suit us than the one we were in, I found myself
sitting in front of the Diocesan Bishop. He spoke about
the development plans, and asked me why I was opposing
them. I opened my mouth, and the words just tumbled
out: "I believe in a God who builds churches, and who
causes them to grow, He doesn't knock them down. I
believe that He wants to fill All Saints church, and He
wants it to be a light to the community, and I believe it
so strongly that I want you to put the development on
hold for two years. Give me free rein to do what seems
right, and if at the end of the two years it hasn't grown,
and you aren't satisfied, then I want you to sack me,
and I will leave the church, because I will have totally
misunderstood who God is and what He wants."

The Diocesan Bishop paused, and then said, "You're on. I
want the congregation lively and vibrant, I want the
building warm and welcoming, and I want the

congregation more than doubled, say 45 regular attenders." I agreed, and we prayed together.

5. Warm and welcoming?

All Saints Church is the size of a large barn. It can seat around 400 people just in the centre two aisles. At that time there were no carpets, no real heating, and no one took their coat off during the services. In fact, in winter the congregation would go over to the church hall and huddle together around a gas heater. The congregation were poor and the revenue of the church came almost entirely from the rental of the hall, and a small house that had been left to them down the road. The entire revenue of the church was little more than a few thousand a year. A bit of a dilemma to say the least. That is why the Diocesan development plan had made so much sense.

Something had to be done about heating the church, not only was it something that the bishop had insisted upon, but also it would be difficult to get new people to come into a building that had ice on the inside of the windows! It was time to call a church council meeting. Actually the council was everyone in the church, and filled the front two pews. We gathered together, one freezing evening near the beginning of November, hats, coats and scarves very much in evidence, to discuss our new plan.

After opening the meeting with a prayer, I asked the council the question, "Do you think that God wants His church to be cold?" We were not going to discuss it, but instead just be quiet and pray about it, and then, in turn, each one say what they thought God was saying. After a minute or two, we went round, and everyone said that they thought that God was saying that He wanted the church warm.

The next day I phoned up British Gas, telling them that we had a church the size of a barn that needed to be heated in time for Christmas. "Can you do it?" I said. "Sir," replied the man "We love a challenge. When can we start?" "Straight away!" I responded. The next week mayhem hit the church. Two lorries and an army of men arrived at the church, then pipes, machines, and soon bits of pew were beginning to fly everywhere. The progress was so pleasing to behold, that is until a passer by popped his head in and said, "Do you have permission to do this?"

6. Not the done thing!

The Church of England is an historic institution, and as such has in its care thousands of unique and important buildings. What makes it unique is that many of these churches are still used for worship. This poses the immediate problem of how to balance the preservation of these ancient buildings with their adaptation for the modern user. To deal with this need, the church has its own kind of planning permission called a 'faculty.' Prior to the alteration of a church building it is common practise to obtain a faculty. This can be quite a lengthy process, involving numerous forms, notices, and of course several committees!

That evening, I phoned up a trusted friend in Devon, who knew all about these things, and he told me that I would definitely need a faculty to undertake the work that we had already begun. Therefore I decided that the next day I would ride my bicycle down to the Diocesan offices, and find out what could be done.

Morning came and I arrived at the Diocesan offices out of breath and more than a little apprehensive about how I was going to be received. I buzzed the buzzer, and found myself face to face with the receptionist. "Can I help you?" she said. "Yes", I replied, "I have come for a faculty."

She gave me a look both of disdain and disbelief, replying, "We don't give out faculties here." "Where do I go to get one then?" I went on to enquire. She then launched on a long diatribe about how you couldn't just walk into the office and get one, you had to fill in a form, which would be looked at by a committee, who would then send out another form to be filled in, followed by another couple of committees, another form, a visit, a period of notice......... I could see that I was going to lose my job before we had even got the place heated at this rate, so I asked, "When we fill in these forms, where do they go?" "The third floor." she replied. I took a deep breath and ran for it.

On the third floor there was a room with computers and smartly dressed people, and a very businesslike air pervading. I said a quick prayer, asking God to grant me favour in their eyes, and charged in, making a speech about the church, and what I believed, saying that if the church was not warm by Christmas I would lose my job. There was a stunned silence. Obviously they were not used to faculty applications being made in this way! All of a sudden the silence broke, and one of them said, "Bob, we would like to help." We filled a form in there and then, and they said that they would rush it through as quickly as possible.

I was so happy that I launched into my next question, "Where is the department of money?" "What do you mean?" The faculty man responded. "Well, I am going to need to money to pay for the work." I stated. "Do you mean that you have started the work and you don't have the money to pay for it?" He said with a mildly alarmed voice. "Bob, you have got everything the wrong way round. You are supposed to obtain a faculty first, then you are supposed to raise the finances, and only after that do you start the actual work."

So I asked them how one went about raising money. They replied that people usually raised it from a mixture of fund raising events, congregational giving and applications to charities. So I asked them where the nearest charity was to where we were talking. They got a huge red book down from the shelf, and found a charity that was two roads away. They then went on to say that I would probably need to make an appointment, and that it might just be a small office that was staffed once a week. I replied that I believed that God was going to give me the money right now, and with that charged down the stairs, past the receptionist, through the door and straight onto my bike.

I arrived at the address of the charity, and buzzed the intercom. To my joy a voice answered, and I sent the whole story of All Saints Church back up through it. There was a silence, and she said that I had better come in.

I fell through the door with my bike, and found myself in a hall with a stairway that seemed to go up for ever. However I had been in such a hurry that I hadn't heard her tell me what floor they were on. So rushing up the stairs I opened the first door that I came to with great enthusiasm, only to find that it was the cleaning cupboard. The cleaning equipment tumbled out, and made its way downstairs with great vigour, the noise ricocheting around the stone walls. I rushed downstairs after a Hoover, only to find that my bicycle had decided to follow me. By the time that I had got everything back into the cupboard, I looked up only to see the entire staff of the charity looking at me from over the banisters.

I walked up, trying to compose myself, and act as if nothing unusual had happened, and upon reaching the top, found myself face to face with a very impressive and smartly dressed gentleman. He invited me into his office. There I poured out my heart to him, all that I believed about what God wanted to do with this run down church in the back streets of Peckham. When I had finished, he looked at me benevolently, and said, "What can we do for you?" "The church is freezing," I replied, "can you give us some money to install a heating system?" "How much do you need?" was his response. I told him the figure, which was several times the yearly income of the church. Then he simply said "O.K. we'll do that." "But" I stammered, don't I have to fill in forms, and doesn't it have to go before a committee?" "Yes", he replied, "But I am the committee, and when we meet in January, it will be approved."

I went back to the church, whistling a merry tune, and asked the firm who were doing the works if they could not bill us until January. They smiled and said that they would 'lose the invoice'. This was just the first in a long line of what some would call coincidences, but I would call 'Godincindences.'

7. Ma Mavis

There are some people in this world who radiate love and light and goodness. They are the unsung heroes who make the world around them a better place. Mavis is one of these people. It turned out that she was behind the Thursday evening prayer meeting, and ran most of the things in the church. She was like the 'church mother,' someone who everyone could go to for a word of advice or encouragement. I still remember many of the things that she said to me: words of encouragement, behind which lay a depth of wisdom that only the years can bring. Once when we were really struggling, pressed in on all sides by opposition and disbelief, I went to her and poured my heart out. She simply responded, "When life pushes you, push Jesus. He's big, He can take it." It has stood me in good stead ever since.

When we first arrived at All Saints, she wasn't around. She had gone 'home', which for Mavis was Jamaica, 'her island' as she called it. I couldn't understand when people said to me, "Wait till you meet Mavis." As the weeks went by, I began to be filled with curiosity. Who was this Mavis? People didn't really tell me anything about her, just that I would really like her. At last the week came when she returned, on a Tuesday afternoon, as I remember it. I thought that we ought to give her a few days to get over jet lag, before visiting her. However by the time Thursday came, I couldn't wait any more. "Come on Jane," I said, "Let's go round and meet this Mavis." So we got in our car, and went round to her house. It was a large terraced house, with a huge Christmas tree growing in the front garden. How I would grow to love that tree!

We drew up outside her house, went up to her front porch and rang the bell. We hadn't told her we were coming; we hadn't even spoken to her. So two perfect strangers were suddenly met with the kindest face nearly split in half with the biggest smile on the planet. She invited us into her front room and told us about what she believed, and how that summer they had held a final church meal in the church hall, before it was to be demolished. A sort of 'Last Supper.' At the end of the meal she got up and made a speech about how this would not be the last meal in the hall, and how it was not going to be knocked down, because God was bigger than that.

Mavis became a real source of strength for us, as straight and true a friend as anyone could ever hope to have. She and her band of helpers, my 'praying ladies' as I called them, were the backbone of the church, and supported me every step of the way.

Later on, when the church started to grow, from twenty, to forty, to eighty, to one hundred and ten, to well over three hundred, when it was overflowing with students, and young professional people, I always insisted that the praying ladies should have a place on the church council. Once, one of the newcomers came up to me and said, "Why do you have all these elderly Caribbean ladies in leadership, shouldn't the council be more representative of the make up on the church." To which I replied, "if it wasn't for them, you wouldn't have a church to come to."

8. Roasting the committee

You may remember that the bishop had agreed to
suspend the redevelopment plan for the site for a period
of two years, on the condition that the church building
was warm and welcoming and that the congregation
had grown from twenty to forty. The Archdeacon was
still very keen on the plan, and considerable money
had already been spent with a very expensive firm of
architects from the City. Therefore I was a little taken
back when he phoned me up to tell me that he was going
to have a meeting with some representatives from that
firm in the church in three weeks time, to continue with
their discussions. As far as they were concerned, what
we believed and had agreed with the bishop was just a
temporary set back in their plans.

Meanwhile, back at the church, the heating systems
was just a few days away from completion. By this time
it was late November, and the building was beginning
to plummet down to its usual sub-arctic temperature!
People were beginning to add bobble hats and scarves to
their Sunday attire. (You have to remember it just doesn't
get this cold in the Caribbean!) I remember announcing
that Sunday that the next week we were going to be warm,
to which a shout of 'hallelujah' went up, and Mavis left
her pew and did a little dance in the aisle. On that day

we made a pact, she and I, that when the church was saved, we would dance together, that was to be one of the sweetest dances in my life, me and this seventy year old grandma dancing together before hundreds of people, many of them not knowing why – but we did and God did, for it was to His music that we danced.

That Friday, British Gas took their leave. I had asked them to provide a system that would enable the church to be a warm as an oven. As he left, the chief engineer said to me, "I hope that you have your Christmas turkey Rev., because your oven is ready."

That evening Jane and I laughed about the Church being an oven, and the congregation needing to come in their bathing suits instead of in hats and scarves. It must have gone round and round in my mind whilst I was asleep, because I awoke with an idea. This rather smart committee were coming round to discuss the redevelopment of the soon-to-be-demolished church, and its site. Their memory of it was a group of disheartened people and a cold damp building. Therefore it stood to reason that they would be coming well dressed for winter weather, so I decided to 'cook them' in my new oven.

I turned all the heaters on full blast, cancelled the timers and left them going, twenty four hours a day, for the entire week. By Sunday, it was lovely and warm, and really made a difference to how people were feeling. Something concrete had changed. People's faith levels began to grow. By Thursday it was unbearable. Friday morning I waited for the archdeacon and the architects to arrive. I placed chairs in a semi-circle round one of the heaters.

A knock came at the door, and I innocently welcomed them in. suggesting that they sat in the chairs around the heater. They willingly obliged, one of them remarking on how cold this building had been on their last visit. I went off to make them some coffee, watching them from a distance. It took them a couple of minutes to work out what was happening, then all of a sudden the first one cracked, taking off his hat and scarf, then his coat. Soon every coat was off, and they began to get to work on their jumpers. The Archdeacon the said, "It's rather hot in here." To which I replied, tongue in cheek, "Would you like me to turn the heating down a little."

Then it happened. Half way through the meeting, one of the partners of this high powered firm suddenly said, "This church was supposed to be dead." At this point I made what I believed very plain and his response was, "this church is not going to be pulled down." Soon after that, the meeting finished. This church was alive, it was the development plans that had died.

9. The 'Change' Word

The church people were certainly alive, but the building itself looked very dead. The notice board was covered by bushes that had got completely out of hand. The building looked dark and dismal, with pigeons flying in and out of the bell tower. The vicarage was behind the Church, and was unoccupied, and behind that lay the huge dilapidated hall. The hall was full of dry rot, with broken windows, and daylight coming through the roof in several places. It had been broken into several times and vandalised. We had been cautioned by the firm of architects that we could no longer use the one room that we were using, and renting out, because the roof was in such a state and pitched at such an angle, that a slate could easily fall of, "and decapitate someone" as he put it. Therefore we had to lose a large part of the church's very small income, and rope the hall building off from that time onwards.

The truth is that the building looked as if it had been closed down for years. No new person would ever think of venturing in there. One day I decided to stand at the end of the road to speak to people about the church, and to my surprise, discovered that the local people didn't know that there was still a church that met there.

It was just as well that no one did venture in, because the shape of the service was singularly unattractive. The entire service came out of a book, actually people were handed several books as they walked through the door. People sat down for an hour, followed a computer printed service order and read from books. The whole thing was very dull, and totally dependant upon the vicar. The congregation, with all their life and colour, had no real way of expressing their faith.

I remember taking a walk down the high street in Peckham, and looking at the shops, and the sort of people who lived there. There were no book shops, or smart organised shops of any kind. (Someone told me that Marks and Spencer had once opened a store there, but had since pulled out.) All this caused me to ask the question, "Who is this church for?" It certainly didn't meet the people in the neighbourhood where they were. The feeling welled up in me that we needed to rethink how we were doing church, and who we were doing it for.

There are many emotive words that you can say to various groups of people to evoke a reaction of terror. Exactly what word you use depends upon the group that you want to shock. In the case of the Church of England the appropriate word would be 'Change!' The Victorians had a rhyme:

Like a mighty tortoise, moves the Church of God,
Brothers we are treading, where we've always trod!

And very little has changed since that rhyme's writing.
However something was about to change at All Saints.

That Sunday I called a meeting after the service, and
said to the people that I believed we needed to change
the way we worshipped on Sunday, and I asked them if
they would trust me and let me change whatever I felt
needed to be changed, for a period of six months. After
this time we could review it, and if it was working we
would continue with the changes, if not we could always
change back to the old way of doing things. This was a
key moment, upon their decision hung more than they
could know. It is true to say that over ninety percent of
the churches that I have visited would have answered no
to that. Yet at All Saints they were very gracious, and
said that I could change what I liked. I changed
everything. One person left, and went to a local church
that was more traditional. Within six months the
congregation had doubled.

10. The first new member

Although there was a vicarage on site, we were not
allowed to move into it. We had asked to live there,
but were not allowed to. We had been told that this
was because it was dangerous. We were told it was a
violent area, and the house was not overlooked, so there
would be 'no one to hear us scream.' Instead we were
moved into a terraced house, near a park about seven
miles away, in someone else's parish. It wasn't even in
the same deanery. I believe that the real reason that we
were prevented from moving in there was because of the
planned demolition and redevelopment of the site. You
can't do that sort of work with a young family living in
the middle of it. However the 'no one to hear you scream'
argument would come in very useful at a later date!

It is very difficult to build up a community- based church
if you are not living in the community. So although we
weren't allowed to move into the vicarage that was next
to the church, it was possible for me to have a study there.
So I moved all my books and things into the vicarage, and
I was so glad that I had, because it was there that we got
our first new member. I remember the day well. I was
sitting in my study, thinking about what I was going to
say on Sunday when the doorbell went. I opened the door
only to find a thin young African man standing there

holding out a sort of tray. It rather reminded me of the ice cream trays that the ladies in the cinema used to bring round during the interval. I greeted the man and asked him what I could do for him and to my surprise, he asked me if I wanted to buy some perfume!

At first I thought that it was a practical joke, then wondered if the member of the congregation who had left because she didn't like the new style of services had told someone that the vicar smells! But no, he was for real. So I bought some perfume, and invited him to church. To my surprise, that Sunday, he came. The next week he came again, and soon he joined us. He always seemed so grateful, although we hadn't really done anything for him. It rather surprised me when he came up to me one Sunday and said that he wouldn't be in church for the next two weeks. When I asked him why, he told me that he was going running. I thought no more of it until he returned back to church. He just didn't seem to be his usual self. He just looked low. I asked him what was wrong, and he replied that he didn't run very well, I tried to console him, telling him not to worry. Then it just slipped out, "where did you finish in your race?" "Fifteenth," he replied. "Well I'm sure that fifteenth isn't too bad; fifteenth out of how many?" I asked. "Fifteenth out of fifty thousand." He replied glumly. This little African man, from the back streets of Peckham had just run a marathon, The Great North Run, and beaten nearly fifty thousand people.

11. A Speaker system for the hordes

Faith is the ability to see beyond what the majority see, to see not what is likely to happen, but rather to see what is possible in God's strength. The congregation may have been small in number, but they were big in faith. We believed that the Lord could fill All Saints Church. Everyone told me that this was not possible. The theologians told me that there was no reason why God would want to fill this church as there were plenty of others around it that were half empty. The sociologists told me that it could not fill because people in this social group did not naturally meet in large numbers. Financially we were not viable, and our buildings were in a terrible state of repair. There was no large successful church sponsoring us with finances or resources, and there was no church plant. All we had were the few people who were there and a huge pile of faith.

The first council meeting had approved the heating system, without having the money to pay for it. The second meeting was even wilder!

As far as I was concerned, the Lord was going to fill His church. I had staked my job on it. So it seemed to be important to be ready for all the people who were going to arrive. It was important that people were warm, and this was now taken care of. The next thing was to enable the people in the rear pews to be able to hear. (The fact that at that moment we hardly filled the front two pews hadn't really crossed my mind.) Therefore I decided that we needed to go out and buy a microphone system.

On the day of the next P.C.C. meeting, Jane and I went into Brixton and parked our car round the corner from a shop that sold musical instruments. We went into the shop and the owner came up to us and asked if he could help. I told him that we needed a P.A. system. He asked us what it was for. I replied that it was for a church. What he said next was like a red rag to a bull. "Well if it is for a church then you won't need very much." I said. "I think that you have misunderstood me. Because it is for a church we will need the very best that you have, because only the best is good enough for my God."

So much of what the church uses is second rate. Cold buildings, broken chairs, scrappy photocopied pieces of yellow paper and vehicles that struggle to pass their M.O.T.s I have always believed that we should do and be the best that we can for God, and believe He will to provide what we can't.

The man was a little taken back by my response, but invited us to follow him up to the 'High Tec' room.

Upstairs we entered what can only be described as a 'shrine to sound.' There in front of us was every conceivable size and shape of loudspeaker imaginable. The salesman, pointed out a pair of loudspeakers, which he assured us would be more than adequate for a church. It was then that I spied an awesome pair of loudspeakers in the far corner of the room. I asked him about them, and he said that speakers like those were used by full touring bands. I decided that they would be good enough for a church, and asked him to get them ready, together with an amplifier, mixing desk, and microphones, whilst I brought my car round to the front of the shop to pick it all up. As I turned to go back down the stairs, he said, "Excuse me sir, but how are you going to pay for the equipment?" "Oh, I'm not going to," I replied quite innocently. "I beg your pardon," he replied. "Well," I explained, "first I have to try the equipment out to make certain that it is good enough, then I need to pray and ask God if He wants us to have it, then I need to put it before the P.C.C. tonight." This was obviously a new situation to him. He thought for a second, then said, "This is London, not Devon." "Yes," I replied, "but you know where I live and work!" He thought again, and said "O.K. go on then." So we left a shop with thousands of pounds of equipment, without having paid for it. The afternoon was spent setting up the equipment ready for the P.C.C. that evening.

Evening came and it was cold outside, but the church was like an oven, of course. The same twenty people, who had given the go ahead for the heating system were sitting in the front pew, waiting for what would happen this time. P.C.C. meetings were never boring! I began the meeting with a prayer, and then pointed out the equipment – not that they could have missed it. I then switched it on, and spoke through the microphone, so that they could hear it in action. I explained that the Lord was going to fill His church, and it would be important that people at the back could hear.

You have to remember that this was all with the eyes of faith; at that time, the entire congregation could fit in the front two pews. "We need to ask God if He wants us to have this equipment or not." I said. Then we all reflected for a moment, and I went round everyone in turn asking them what God had said.

Everyone agreed that we should have it, that is until we got to the last person, who said, "Yes, it would be good to have it, but who was going to pay for it?" There was a silence and then the strangest thing in the world happened: an elderly woman put her hand up, and said, "I'll pay for it. I'm am half deaf, and that is the first thing that I have heard in this church for over a decade." And she was as good as her word and paid for it

This became the norm for the church, one miracle after another, with the people of God pulling together around a common vision, to fill the church and save it from closing.

12. Things take their toll

All Saints church was very much alive, but you wouldn't believe it from the look of the place from the outside. Overgrown plants covered the dirty dilapidated notice board, which could have read 'All Saints rubbish tip' from the amount of rubbish; broken furniture, rusty shopping trolleys and the like that filled the front garden. We decided to set to work and cut down all the overgrown plants from the front of the church, replaced the notice board with a new one which advertised our new services – 'All Saints Church, 10.30am All-age service, Lively, Informal and Friendly. Everyone Welcome'. All of a sudden, it no longer looked like it had been closed for decades. Then slowly but surely, the church started to grow and by the end of six months, we already had over forty five members, which was over double what we had started with - and the exact number that the bishop had given us as a target for the end of two years. People came from everywhere in the area, and from all walks of life. Everyone who came through the front door was treated as if they were the most important and special person to have ever walked into the building, and so they were! If they came a second week, then they would be sure to join.

There were many stories of how people came to be drawn to All Saints. One person had just been sitting on a train, and when it pulled into the station that overlooked the church, just felt God telling her to go to church. She came that Sunday and the next week brought five friends. It was exciting, every service was different. People remarked that they didn't want to go away on holiday in case they missed something, and I was right in there with them. I didn't take days off and I didn't take holidays. The church continued to grow, week by week, until by the end of the second year we had over a hundred regular church attenders. However I hadn't realised just how tired I was getting, and at this point the job was only supposed to be half time, with the other half spent helping the other vicars in the deanery. It happened that one day I simply couldn't get off of the sofa. I simply had no energy at all.

When the congregation heard, some of them came round to see me and said that they would like us to take a holiday. They asked us where we would like to go and I replied that we had always wanted to visit Italy. Over the next few days the strangest thing happened, people started posting Italian Lira through our front door. Soon we had enough to go on holiday for a couple of weeks. Yet another example of the practical love and kindness that cemented the church fellowship together.Whilst we were in Italy, I felt that it would be right to ask God to give me a helper in the church. So started the amazing story of how we got our church staff.

13. Two is better than one

I have always loved music, listening to it and playing it. One day we decided to buy ourselves a new C.D. player so we chose a shop and waited to be served. Presently a smart and athletic looking young man came up to us and asked us if he could help. We explained what we were looking for and he took us into a demonstration room, where he brought in player after player, keen for us to hear the difference between them. He did it with dedication, even passion, and more important still, my wife noticed that he was wearing a 'fish badge' on his jacket. These sorts of badges are usually worn by committed Christians, who want other Christians to know that they are believers and also hope that unchurched people might notice the unusual shape and ask what the badge means.

The salesman went out to bring in yet another machine, and while he was out, Jane leant towards me and said, "If he loves God as much as he loves Hi Fi, you need to get him." The poor unsuspecting man came back into the room, and I said, "Do you mind if I ask you something?" He replied, "Not at all, fire away." He was probably expecting a question about music, but that is not what he got. "Do you love God as much as you love Hi Fi?" was my question. "Yes, as a matter of fact, I do." He replied.

"Then leave your job and come and work with me." This was definitely not what he was expecting.

We told him about what the Lord was doing in the church in London, and how he could be a part of it. We also told him that we would only be able to pay him pocket money, a fraction of what he was earning in the shop where he was working. However in spite of this, he said that he wanted to come up to London and see the church. A couple of weeks later, he did just that, and within a couple of months, he had moved into the vicarage. He could not only preach and evangelise, but also he was extremely practical. He was a real help and encouragement to me, and stayed with us for nearly three years.

The next person I needed was an administrator. This came in an even more dramatic form at the Christmas candlelit service. The church was quite full and there was a lady sitting about a third of the way back, with lovely long hair. It was half way through my sermon that it happened. Her hair must have got too close to the candle on the pew behind, because all of a sudden it caught fire. I noticed it before anyone else, and exclaimed from the pulpit, "Either we are having a re run of Pentecost or that lady is on fire!" People around her patted the fire out and amazingly she was unhurt. However she rededicated her life to God and soon after became my administrator.

This lady too experienced the amazing provision of God through His people. She was a single parent mum, with a mortgage on a flat which had become a negative equity. The point had been reached that she was no longer able to pay and the bank was going to foreclose. However even after selling her flat, she was still going to owe a considerable sum of money. She spoke to Jane during one of the mums' bible studies and explained the situation. Everyone felt that she should just stand up at the front of the church and tell it how it was. This was something that was going to require a lot of courage, but she agreed. That Sunday she stood up and said what had happened, and told of the mistakes she had made. I felt it right to have a collection for her and her alone that day. The baskets went round, and everyone gave generously, students, the elderly, those who had little money. At the end of the service she left with a carrier bag with thousands of pounds in, much in the form of IOUs. She rang the bank the next day, told them what had happened, and they said that they would accept the money that she had raised, and write the rest of the debt off.

Next I decided that we would need someone to help with the students. There was a group of three students who had started coming to All Saints, who lived in a house round the corner. One of them, a really intelligent young man, who had just graduated from L.S.E. with a first class degree, had caught my attention. We arranged to go out for a pizza together and it was there that I asked him if he would like to come and work with me as our 'Director of student ministries.' The truth was that we only had a handful of students at this time, as always it was all seen through the eyes of faith. I remember his response, "But Bob, you don't have any students." "I know," I responded, "but we are soon going to have lots."

He had already been offered a high powered job with a large international company, because of his results. He said that he needed to think about it. A couple of days later, he came back with a yes. He moved into the vicarage with the other young man, and stayed with us for two years. He built up a great student work, and the students literally piled into the church. He now has a high powered job with the government.

The church side of things was now nearly set up, but we needed someone to play the music. As usual, the Lord provided.

There was a young couple who joined us, both teachers – and both musicians. They began to get more involved with the church. They were both a little shy, but lovely people. I spent some time with them, and found that they really felt called to lead the musical side of worship, so I suggested my usual, and asked if the woman would give up being a teacher for a while and look after the church music, and help me with the hall refurbishment. They thought about it, and got back to me with a yes. She was very gifted, as was her husband, and they really brought the church on as they led our worship week after week.

So within a year of being unable to get up from the sofa, God had given me a staff team of four. Over the years this team grew; a lady joined to help start a church school, and a young newly married couple joined to help with the music and young people's work. Another young man gave up his job to join us and actually moved into the vicarage with my family, which in itself was a great act of bravery! He came to manage the church finances and to help organise me. Every time there was a job that needed doing, God brought someone to us, so in all those years, we never placed an advert anywhere for staff - the right people just came along.

14. Our Commitment Tested

There are different levels of commitment, in any project, and sometimes you are put in the position where a little voice inside you asks, "Do you really mean it?" This test can come in many different ways. It came to us in the area of our personal finances. As someone once said, "The last part of a man to be converted is his cheque book!"

The church had grown, and many young families were now beginning to attend. The actual church building was a barn of a place, completely unpartitioned, with stone floors. During the services, the young children had, up to this point, played at the side of the church. However it was now beginning to look and sound like a nursery school. Something had to be done. They could no longer spill out into the vicarage because the staff lived there, and I was unwilling to partition the inside of the building, because I believed that one day it was going to be full, so there was one place left that we could go.......

The church hall was a dilapidated building; dark, damp and full of dry rot, save in the several places where you could actually see large patches of daylight through the roof. It was no longer used for anything. The authorities had made us physically cordon the place off because the pitch of the slate tiles was such that if one should fall off

– which would have been quite possible -, it could have decapitated someone! It was obvious to me that this was the key. We had nowhere for the children to go, nowhere to have social gatherings or for the students to meet. So I put it to the church that we should refurbish the whole building. Everyone thought that it was a great idea, so I went ahead and got estimates. I then approached the diocese for a loan. This was a great challenge for them, because a couple of years before they had expected to rake in quite a few shillings from the development of the plot Therefore the idea of now investing large sums of money into the project was a complete turnaround. However, with great support from the archdeacon, who had originally headed up the idea of selling off the site, the diocese agreed. It was amazing, we could make a start. People really got behind the project, and lots of extra money was raised. The young lady who was leading the music agreed to take responsibility for the project, helped by Jane.

Work started; at first it was slow, but soon gathered momentum. The project grew, and so did the price tag. It soon became obvious that the money we had raised was not going to finish the project. What were we going to do? The church had one asset, a small terraced property on one of the main roads nearby. It was in a bad state of repair, and completely unmodernised, with no fitted kitchen or central heating. Even worse, from a selling point of view, it had three sitting tenants, who paid a very low rent.

We needed to raise money, and raise it quickly. We knew that once contractors start other jobs, you never get them back! Jane and I had a lovely house in Plymouth; we loved it and hoped one day to retire there. However we felt God telling us to sell it and buy the Church house, not something that filled us with delight. So we decided to test this by saying that we would put it on the market, and if it sold in time, which we thought (and hoped!) unlikely, then we would do it. We put the idea to the church council, who agreed and after a valuation, set a price. We tried to get out of buying it by offering it to the tenants, who said that they didn't want to buy it.

You can guess what happened. Our house sold immediately, and we became the proud owners of a run-down house in Peckham with sitting tenants, but the Hall project was able to continue uninterrupted.

We spent a lot of money on the church house, and it was a constant source of worry to us. However over the next 18 months the house prices went up in the area, and the tenants eventually agreed to us selling the place. We accepted an offer that was quite a bit more than we had paid for it, so we decided to pay off our mortgage, buy a new car, and put some money in the bank. This we did, only to find that we felt God telling us to give the money that we had just put in the bank to the church. I remember this being a very hard thing for me to accept. It was a very large sum of money to just give away! However the feeling increased rather than decreased and I had no peace until I agreed, which I did after a sleepless night with the 'flu. The treasurer was delighted.

I have to say that since then we have been given more than we could possibly ever imagine, but at the time I didn't know that this would happen so it was all a big leap of faith.

The hall was opened with a huge party and a jazz band. The archdeacon gave a speech and said that never in his experience had he seen a church so close to disappearing from the planet burst back into life as All Saints had. I had told Ma Mavis that when the hall was refurbished I would dance with her. As the band struck up the first song, I went up to Mavis and asked her for the pleasure of the first dance. We danced and the church cheered.

15. Church Politics!

The Church was really beginning to grow and develop, great news for all concerned in the Christian community, one might be forgiven for thinking. However good news isn't always received in the way that we expect! What you have to remember is that up to this point my post was only supposed to be a half time, winding down affair: not thought to be viable; someone to help in the Deanery whilst overseeing the demolition of the church, vicarage, and hall and the building of a new group of private houses and community hall.

All Saints Church was officially a half time post, with the vicarage not even being in the Deanery, but some seven miles from the church.. In London this is a long way. This was all part of the winding down of All Saints, and the general decline management of the Church of England in general. The problem was that now the reality wasn't matching the expectation! All Saints was growing and changing on a weekly basis. Therefore Jane and I decided that we needed to live nearer to the church, so the Diocese needed to be persuaded to buy a new vicarage, which meant investing money in a project that was supposed to bring in money through its sale. For this to happen we had to suddenly step into a political arena.

As All Saints was a half time post, the first thing that needed to happen was that it should become a full time post. It was made a half time post because it was not considered viable. To change this would mean that the Diocese would have to completely overturn its previous decision, but more than that, the other churches in the Deanery would have to agree. Why would this be a problem? Because they were losing their Deanery Missioner? Not really. The truth was that the job had no real meaning in the Deanery because there was no real consensus as to what the job really was. Anyway, I had ceased to do much for the Deanery once All Saints began to grow. When they had a meeting to discuss the whole matter, only one vicar turned up, and said that he thought that it was a great idea to lose the post of Deanery Missioner. He was a great friend and supporter, and was delighted that no one else turned up!

However there was a deeper reason why other churches might object, and this came to the forefront when we went for the next stage. The first stage had been to make the job full time. The next stage was to get a new vicarage actually in the parish (whilst keeping the old one which was now full up with staff!). In order for this to happen my status needed to change from being that of a Priest-in-charge, to a Freehold post. A priest-in-charge is a five year appointment with little or no security for the church concerned. As such at any time the church could be reorganised, closed, or joined with another church , or two. As a freehold post it was very secure, and had the right to a proper vicarage. The problem is that the Diocese was continually having to cut posts to save money. Every five years or so, a deanery would face losing a post. This is what had happened to All Saints when it had become half time with the formerly full time Deanery Missioner's post. The cuts would come around again, and with All Saints as a full time, freehold post, it would not get cut – one of the other churches, which were by this time far smaller, would go. Needless to say, when I proposed that the freehold be returned to All Saints there was opposition from most of the churches in the deanery.

We were told that we should not push this issue, as we might lose everything if we did. Jane and I felt that we should go for it, all or nothing. For us Faith was spelt RISK! The Church agreed.

We decided to put it to the relevant committees. Influence must have been used because everyone turned us down. Finally we received a letter from the bishop saying that he refused to give us freehold status.

I remember asking Jane what we should do. To my surprise she said, "let's take legal advice." She rang up the diocesan registrar (high powered lawyer type person) and asked him to state the reasons for the suspension of a living. He gave her three reasons. None of these were the case with All Saints, so we asked him to inform the bishop that we would see him in court. A few days later we were given the freehold.

The time had come to go vicarage hunting.

16. The most expensive vicarage ever bought

"But All Saints already has a vicarage,"said the diocesan
property man. "Ah yes," we replied, "but as you yourself
said, it is isolated, dangerous, and unsuitable for a young
family." He then said that there were no houses suitable
as vicarages in the area because they were all tall and
thin and high on maintenance. Apparently the Church
of England doesn't buy tall thin houses. There is a guide
book for vicarages, and this had to be met. So we said:
if we find a suitable one, would he buy it. He said that he
would put it to the committee, which to my surprise said
yes. But we had to find such a house.

Peckham is full of tall thin houses. So Jane and I dressed
smartly and went to a rather upmarket estate agent,
saying that we were looking for a two storey house in
the area at any price. To our surprise they found one,
possibly the only one in the parish. It was fiendishly
expensive. I rang up the property man, who nearly fell
off his perch. He in turn rang up the diocesan negotiator,
who couldn't believe the price, and thought it was
excessive. Two days later the house was sold to someone
else for the full asking price.

A couple of days later, feeling a bit down in the dumps,
Jane and I drove down the road, past the house that we

had missed.. That side of the road was the last road in the parish. What is more it was the only two storey house down the street. However as we drove down the road, we suddenly noticed a similar house on the other side of the road, but it was just outside the parish. It was to our great surprise that a couple of days later we received a call from the estate agents saying that this house was now on the market. So I phoned up the negotiator's firm and asked them to tell him the news, and to tell him that I thought that we were probably wasting our time because in my opinion he was incapable of moving at sufficient speed to buy a house in the current market.

That very afternoon, he went down to the house and bought it. It was one of the most expensive houses that the diocese had ever bought.

17. Letting Go

One of the hardest things that we have to do is to let go. Especially when the thing we are relinquishing is something that our hearts love and our lives have been invested in. It's true of people; we have to let go of our children when they go to college or get married, or just move out to set up their own home. It's also true of places where we have lived, or worked, and projects that we have seen through from the beginning. They are things that we have put ourselves into. It is difficult when you have been called to pioneer things. All the time that we had been at All Saints we had been preparing to leave, making certain that we were laying down foundations that would stand, after we had left. Sometimes a church becomes so dependant upon its leader that when he or she leaves it all falls apart, or regresses. This was something that we always guarded against.

The Church was now the fastest growing Anglican Church in South London, the finances were very healthy indeed, the buildings were refurbished and we had a great staff team. There was a wonderful vicarage and the job had been returned to freehold status. During the last year, the bishop agreed to give us a curate. They sent us a very capable young man, in whose hands I felt confident I could leave the church. We worked with him for a year, by the end of which time we decided our part in God's plan was completed and the time had come to move on. He had sent us there to take it so far, and then to hand it on. Many a thing is spoilt because a person tries to hang onto it for too long, reluctant to let go.

The people didn't want us to move on, but the wonderful thing was that after we had left, the Church continued to develop and grow, and now has a new minister, who continues the good work.

There is a time to hold on and a time to let go. It is hard to let go of a success and step out again into the unknown. Where can you go from a church like All Saints. Perhaps something completely different? A nice stint in the countryside seemed the order of the day. Five rural villages in Wiltshire. A lovely place to live, surrounded by a close, warm, supportive, caring community. Everyone pulling together to grow the church in the countryside.... but that's another story!